STAND OUT

THE TRUE STORY OF PARALYMPIC GOLD MEDALLIST GREG STEWART

A team effort by Greg Stewart and Sean Campbell

Illustrated by Lana Lee

You can do or be whatever you want, just do it!

To Mom & Dad. Thank you for showing Wade, Dean, and myself nothing but love and support. We are extremely proud to call you our parents!   - Greg

To Rhys and Dez. Two of the biggest book lovers I know.

-Sean

More info at www.seancampbellauthor.com

© 2024 Sean Campbell.

All rights reserved. No part of this book may be reproduced in any form without the written permission of the author.

STAND OUT

1. A person of exceptional ability

2. Easily noticeable

This is big Greg Stewart.
He is funny and smart.
Made of muscle and bone,
but most say he's all heart.

He was born with one arm,
this cute little baby.
But he was determined
no if, but, or maybe.

His family was strong.
They taught him to stand.
His parents stayed close
to lend him a hand.

An unpleasant thought in the back of his mind made his cheerful self become harder to find.

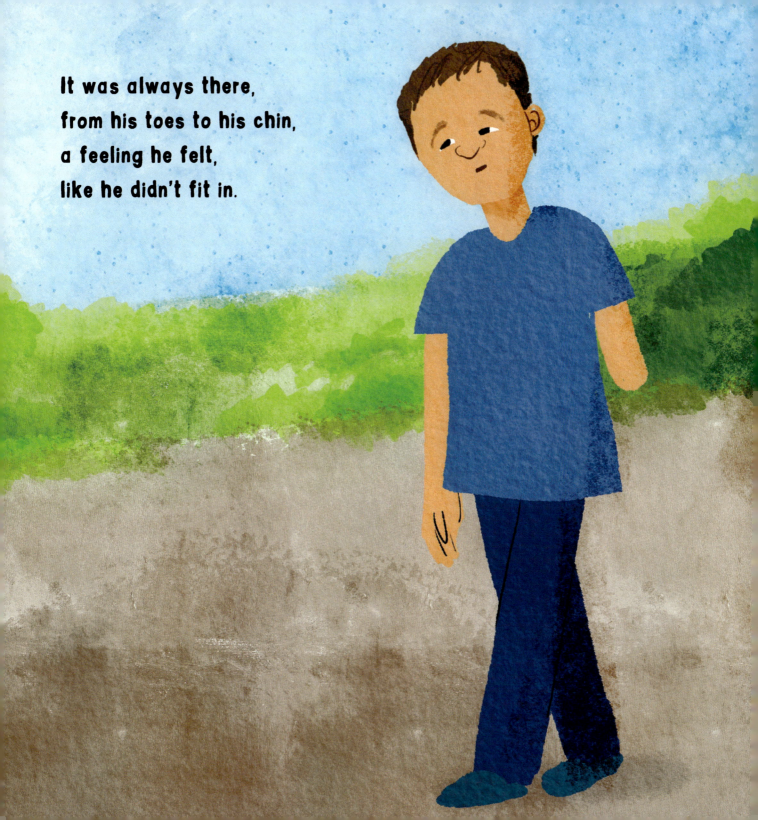

It was always there,
from his toes to his chin,
a feeling he felt,
like he didn't fit in.

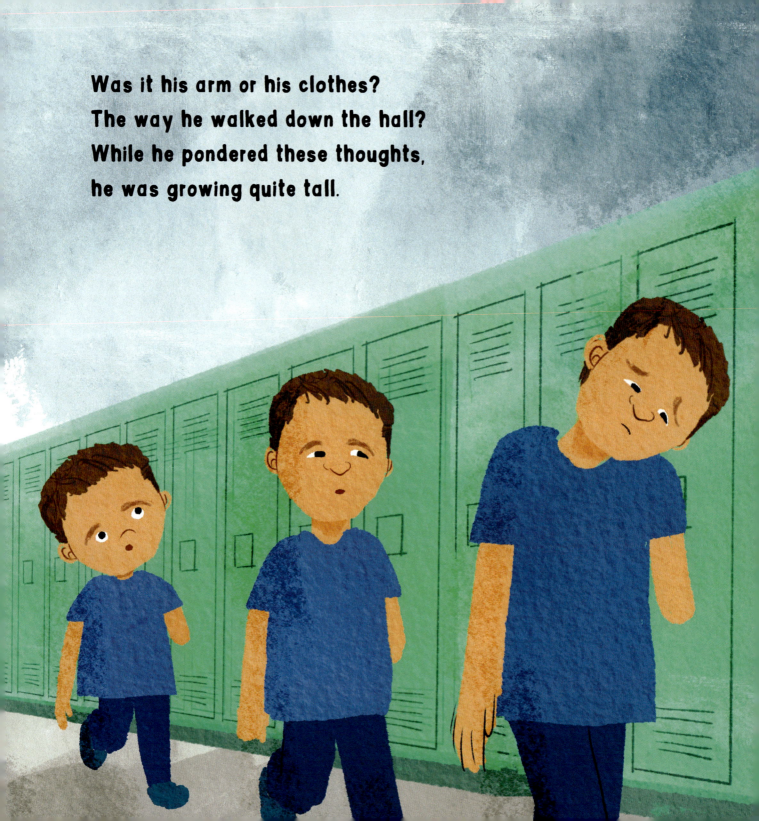

Was it his arm or his clothes?
The way he walked down the hall?
While he pondered these thoughts,
he was growing quite tall.

Whoa, whoa, pump the brakes!
What's this height all about?
Oh, great, here we go,
another way to stand out.

A big part of each team.
His play was devine.
So he should have felt great,
but he wasn't even fine.

Not one to sit back,
Greg sprang into action.
He set out to find
a true human connection.

With their help and support, he felt part of the crew. It was time to move forward and try something new.

To start his next journey, he took up shot put. He got better quickly with an Olympian's input.

After four years of training,
Greg was off to Japan.
He stepped off the plane
into a paralympic wonderland.

There was no cheering crowd, but it didn't dent his pride. The cheers he most needed now rose from inside.

He stepped into the circle
feeling brave, feeling strong.
His throw was so straight.
His throw was so looooooong!

Life is not a straight line,
not always easy, I'm told,
but in his big moment...

Greg shone bright as gold.

In 2021, Greg Stewart represented Canada at the Paralympic Summer Games in Japan, where he won a gold medal in the shot put. His first mighty throw was a paralympic record of 16.75 meters. There was no crowd permitted at these Paralympic Games because of the COVID-19 pandemic. Greg cheered himself and his fellow athletes on instead.

"I am honoured to share some of Greg's life journey and witness his unwavering determination firsthand. Just being around him, feeling his selfless spirit and his strength of character, will make you believe that anything is possible."

-Carla Nicholls
Para Performance Lead,
Athletics Canada

Greg, and his fiance Taylor, live and laugh in beautiful British Columbia. He is an amazing public speaker who uses his unique personal story to inspire students and corporate groups.

Manufactured by Amazon.ca
Bolton, ON